Margie,

May you always live life to the fullest!

Samantha

Ginormous, Outrageous, Audacious Living

· ·

what's your **GOAL?**

Ginormous, Outrageous, Audacious Living

●●●●●●●●●●●●●●●●●●●●●●●●●●

what's your GOAL?

Samantha Murchek

Published by Masvoli Publishing

Edited by Peggy Davidson

Stylist, Amy Beaman

Dallas, Texas

Ginormous, **O**utrageous, **A**udacious Living! What's Your **GOAL**?

Samantha Murchek

Copyright © by Samantha Murchek. All rights reserved. Written permission must be secured from the author to use or reproduce any part of this book, except for occasional page copying for personal study.

All scripture quotations are taken from *The Holy Bible*, New International Version®. Copyright 1973, 1978, 1984 by International Bible Society.

Any emphases or comments within Scripture are the author's own.

ISBN: 1452869081

Contents

Acknowledgements vii
Introduction xi

1	Our Experiences Shape Us	1
2	The Things That Nobody Tells You	5
3	What Is Your Ginormous Goal?	15
4	Outrageous Enthusiasm!	27
5	Audacious: Overcoming Fear and Intimidation	35
6	Living in a Circle of Influence	43
7	Focusing Forward	55
8	Predictors of Success	63
9	Paying It Forward	71
10	Your Unwritten Chapter	77
	SMART Goal Sheets	83
	Tear-Out Daily Inspirations	89
	Gifts, Skills, Abilities Worksheet	125
	Circle of Influence Worksheet	129
	Notes	133

Acknowledgements

Writing a book is an amazing adventure like no other. I thank my wonderful family, friends and countless women who shared their perspective and opinions with me. It brings me such joy to have such a brilliant network of people surrounding me. God gave me the words to write, the stories to share and the remarkable people to bring this book to life. It is with tears of gratitude that I single out a few people.

To Mary Kay Ash, a woman who made much of little. I also thank Mary Kay Inc. and the millions of beautiful women in the U.S. and worldwide who continue to perpetuate Mary Kay Ash's dream by enriching women's lives around the world. I thank all of you for raising me in this family for 14 years and teaching me life changing lessons while demonstrating what reaching for the stars looks like. I am eternally grateful for my time with you.

ACKNOWLEDGEMENTS

To Todd Birdsong for his heart of gold and generosity. Thank you for giving me the tools to write this book, literally.

To Peggy Davidson for countless hours of editing while keeping the intention of the book pure. You are a woman of sincere character, integrity and strength and I could not have completed this book without you! I am forever grateful!

To my Bible Study Beauties. Thank you for your courage and the humble hearts you bring each week as we continue seeking and learning our Father's word. You've inspired me and provided examples for others to follow. Your constant encouragement, bold prayers and stories have been instrumental in making this book come to life. I thank you for sharing your stories openly and honestly even when there was question as to what stories may appear in print. I hope you are now at peace.

To Beth Landsberg for helping me uncover true authenticity. We've been through peaks and valleys together and we stand strong and united as women on this journey of living God's best life. My heart is full of gratitude for your unconditional love! Thirteen years of friendship and memories and I know we will create many more in the years to come. Thank you for your invaluable time to review this book and ensuring that my voice was heard. You're a true diamond in the rough. I love you friend.

To Susan Evans, Sharon Reedie and Amy Beaman for your genuine interest in bringing the best out in this book. Your gifts of time and talent are remarkable and forever cherished.

To all of my wonderful girlfriends who came to my book brunch to shed light on every chapter discussed in this book. I am blessed to have such wonderful, beautiful, intelligent women in my life who care so much about others.

To my phenomenal husband Ron, who had no idea what he was getting himself into by marrying a woman with ginormous goals. No words can come close to expressing my gratitude for your encouragement, your energy, your ideas and your love. You've shown me what true love looks like and you've been a huge inspiration for this book. Your generosity continues to enrich my life every day. I am truly blessed to have someone as wonderful as you in my life. I am excited to continue our ginormous, outrageous, audacious life together! You're the macaroni to my cheese!

Introduction

This book is designed to help you discover all of the gifts that you have been uniquely designed with, and to move forward experiencing a life that is so much more than you have ever dreamed or imagined. I've discovered that the first step to fully understanding your unlimited potential and greatness requires an open mind, heart and soul in addition to allowing yourself to let go of past hurts and failures.

We all have past hurts and failures, but I am here to tell you that there is hope. No matter your age or past, it is never too late to fulfill your destiny. Please stick with me over these pages to see that sometimes during the most trying moments, may it be divorce, losing your job or falling short of your expectations and goals, that good things are to come for you. As Romans 8:28 states, "And we know that in all things God works for the good of those who love him, who have been called according to his purpose." God wants greatness for you and I, and it brings immense joy when we live out the life He has designed us to live.

I've been a part of helping over 1.7 million women worldwide overcome challenges, work through fears, accomplish goals and achieve a life bigger than they could've dreamed. By sharing my life experience with you, my prayer is that you discover that when God closes a door He opens a window. The best lies ahead for you; it's yours for the taking.

In this book I will share with you some of my experiences, including the things that no one tells you – from the ugly to the joyful, the fearful to the courageous, the unworthy to the bold. I admit in doing this I feel somewhat vulnerable, as if I'm standing on a stage naked in front of thousands! But if my embarrassing experiences can help just one of you realize that you're not alone then it is worth revealing every one of those moments. It's in these defining moments that our true character is developed.

I reassure you that God has great plans for you, and you are worthy of greatness. If you picked up this book you are already on your way. I challenge you to step out of your comfort zone and step into the Ginormous, Outrageous, Audacious Life that awaits you!

> *Examine yourself; discover where your*
> *True chance of greatness lies.*
> *Seize that chance and let no power or*
> *Persuasion deter you from your task.*
>   *Schoolmaster in Chariots of Fire*

Chapter 1

Our Experiences Shape Us

I grew up in a very small town in Wisconsin, a town where everyone knew everyone. In summertime the kids would play softball together for hours. One of my earliest goal-achieving memories, although I didn't know what a goal was at that point, was to win first place in our summer softball league. I was in grade school and played on an all-girls team. I was the pitcher, my sister played in the outfield, and my mother was the assistant coach. My sister and I, only a year apart, were very competitive. Can you sense the storm brewing?

Our team played great and we found ourselves headed toward the final tournament competing for first place. We had worked hard and were ready for our final game. The sun was shining, the parents were in the bleachers cheering and the final championship game began. Inning after inning we battled to pull ahead. The tension was building between the teams and between my sister and me. If you asked her, she would tell you she was "encouraging" me, but in the last inning of the game I finally had enough of her "encouragement." All eyes were on me as I readied for my next pitch, but instead I threw down my glove, walked out to my sister and explained to her, not so subtly, that her "encouragement" was NOT NEEDED! As I finished my explanation, I vividly remember catching a glimpse of my mother as she was shaking her head while hiding behind one of the bleachers pretending that she didn't know either of us.

I walked back to the pitcher's mound and threw the final pitch that struck out the batter. We won the game, captured first place and I received the MVP (most valuable player) award. I was so excited! I couldn't wait for the awards ceremony so I could pick up my MVP trophy. The awards ceremony began, and they handed out the first-, second- and third-place trophies. Next was the MVP award. I had envisioned a place for this trophy in my room where I (and my sister) could see it! I anxiously waited to hear my name so I could claim my fame, my trophy, my prize. Finally they called Most Valuable Player, Samantha Sommerfeld, and I ran out onto the field to receive my CAN OF SODA! Yes, a can of soda. That moment marked one of the first major disappointments in my life. To this day I still remember that feeling of loss and pain in the pit of my stomach.

It was devastating. The boys baseball league awarded MVP trophies so I expected one too. A can of soda! It just didn't make sense to me! My poor mom had quite a job of trying to calm my frustration, disappointment and heartbreak over the next several days.

I am sure you can relate, in one way or another, to this story. Every one of us experiences disappointments, losses or unexpected challenges in life. We get our hopes up, we believe in something whole-heartedly and we give it everything that we've got. When we are met with unfair circumstances or challenges, what do we do? How do we handle it? Where do we turn? How do we move forward?

A few months ago I experienced another one of those disappointing moments. My world as I had known it for over a decade had changed in one tiny sentence: "Your position has been eliminated."

After 14 years in corporate America, I lost my job. Up to this point I believed that you followed the path of graduating high school and university and then found a safe and secure job with benefits where you remained until retirement. I believed that this was the ultimate "success story."

I am grateful for my time in corporate America, but I believe it can change you. As the years passed, I began to conform to the job and politics. I focused solely on the company and achieving its goals and began losing sight of the gifts, talents, dreams and visions that God gave me.

In 1 Peter 4:10 we are told that, "Each one should use whatever gift he has received to serve others, faithfully administering God's grace in its various forms." In corporate America, on the other hand, the goal is to be good in all areas instead of focusing on your specific gifts. You are given your review and told your "areas of opportunities" instead of focusing on your gifts.

My point: Remain authentic to the gifts God gave you. I like Dan Miller's philosophy:[1]

- Work where you are the strongest 80 percent of the time.
- Work where you are learning 15 percent of the time.
- Work where you are weak 5 percent of the time.

Chapter 2
The Things That Nobody Tells You

Unfortunately nobody tells you what happens after a significant loss. That loss may be a marriage, a loved one, a friendship or a job. Experiencing losses in life are very painful and can be equally as painful to move beyond. However, with time, these losses can be eye-opening experiences that reveal new opportunities and seasons of growth and abundance. If we can look back at our losses and pull a few lessons or memories forward, this time of grieving and reflection can be one of the most enlightening times in our lives.

What I've realized about significant losses is that we typically cycle through the same emotional stages. Whether we are grieving the loss of a marriage, a loved one, a friendship or a job, it leaves us asking ourselves many questions: What on earth am I going to do? Who am I? What am I good at? What is my purpose?

For me and my recent job loss, I found myself replaying the negativity in my head like a bad movie. Who was I now? I had no title, no significance and no contribution. My entire career was dedicated to helping hundreds of thousands of women across the world achieve their goals, enriching their lives and now my cup was left completely and utterly empty. No one ever told me I would feel this way. I remember experiencing these same types of emotions through other losses in my life.

Nearly everyone experiences loss: a marriage, a loved one, a job, a friendship. If you have experienced any type of loss, my desire is that you find your way to move forward into a life that is full of joy and peace. And that you find that the time between the loss and moving forward is one of rest, reflection and transformation. And it can be, IF you take time to grieve what you have lost, whatever that loss is for you.

> *Consider it pure joy, my brothers, whenever you face trials of many kinds, because you know that the testing of your faith develops perseverance. Perseverance must finish its work so that you may be mature and complete, not lacking anything.*
> *James 1:2-4*

> *When you get into a tight place and everything goes against you, till it seems as though you could not hold on a minute longer, never give up then, for that is just the place and time that the tide will turn.*
> **Harriet Beecher Stowe**

> *Blessed is the man who perseveres under trial, because when he has stood the test, he will receive the crown of life that God has promised to those who love him.*
> **James 1:12**

A friend of mine, Sharon, is a partner in a firm specializing in career transition consulting. She has the following to say about significant losses: "Job loss is not unlike the grieving process experienced in the loss of a loved one. It is important that you allow yourself to experience these emotions – they are normal and healthy. Almost any major change in life is accompanied by some anxiety. Your self-identity is inherently tied to your job; hence your self-identity has been struck a severe blow! Additionally, the affiliations with co-workers, the contribution and value you brought to the organization and even the security of routine are now lost. This adds fuel to the fire of diminishing self-worth. Isn't it logical that you would experience a combination of emotions?"

Research studies have shown significant emotional similarities between job loss and the grieving process associated with the loss of a loved one. Elisabeth Kubler-Ross studied these emotional stages:

1. Denial
2. Anger
3. Bargaining
4. Depression
5. Acceptance

Further studies by Louis Ferman applied the Kubler-Ross concepts to the emotions experienced with job loss as follows:

- Relief
- Panic
- Shock
- Depression
- Denial
- Resignation
- Anger
- Acceptance
- Bargaining
- Building
- Guilt
- Growth

Although your loss may not be a career loss but rather a marital loss or loss of a friendship or loss of a loved one, these same stages apply. No matter what your loss is, it is important to walk through these stages fully and allow the healing to begin. Let me share with you my experience of job loss as I went through these emotional stages recently.

1. **Denial:** not accepting or even acknowledging the loss; pretending it is a bad dream and it will go away. You can't believe this is happening to you.

   When I was first told that my position was eliminated, I was in absolute shock! After the numbness wore off and feeling slowly returned into my chest, arms, legs and remaining body parts, I started crying. And crying. And crying. Then I cried some more.

2. **Anger:** wanting to fight back or get even. During this time you may waiver back and forth between denial and anger. You may be angry toward your former boss or co-workers. You may take out your anger on those closest to you without even realizing it.

   I'm not an angry person but I excelled in this area for quite some time. I was so angry about everything from my loyalty to their disloyalty. Mostly I felt angry about being betrayed.

3. **Bargaining:** attempting to make deals to stop or change the loss.

   I was given some time before my official last day with the company to wrap up some projects. During this time I waivered back and forth in hopes that a different position within the company would open up for me. Maybe I really didn't have to leave? I'd been with this company for 14 years and knew everyone, right?

4. **Depression:** overwhelming feelings of hopelessness, frustration, bitterness, self-pity; mourning loss of hopes, dreams and plans for the future.

I had deep sadness in my heart and soul. I felt utter loss and failure. Was it something I said or did? Wasn't I good enough? I had no idea what life was supposed to look like after this loss, and I certainly did not want to tell my family and friends what happened - how embarrassing! I just wanted to crawl back into a ball and stay there forever!

5. **Acceptance:** finding the good that can come out of the pain of loss; finding comfort and healing. Our goals turn toward personal growth.

After a few weeks and reading some great books from Dan Miller and Dave Ramsey, I began to feel hopeful. What was in store for me next? The excitement began to fill my body like the adrenaline rush of skydiving. I began to believe that I learned all that I was supposed to in corporate America and now I was being used for a greater good. I began looking forward.

Don't be alarmed if you discover that it's not a

"straight shot" through these emotions! You may progress through denial, anger, bargaining and one day you realize you're back at anger. This is quite normal. You are still making progress. You might even cycle through these stages several times! Trust me, I know this process well! Just when I thought I was in the acceptance stage something triggered an emotion and I found myself still a little angry. This surprised me. The wonderful news is that there is hope, and it does get better.

Once I allowed myself to fully grieve I rediscovered my gifts, abilities and dreams. This was one of the most exciting times in my life. I read books; I talked with family and friends to find out what I liked to do as a little girl and what I was good at. My mother reminded me that I had the "gift of gab." I began writing down ideas that filtered into my head throughout the day and night. I began to dream again, but bigger than ever before. This was when I was able to move forward. I began to write my goals.

Whether you are exploring self-improvement activities, new hobbies, new interests, a new career path or wanting a new beginning, it is important that you allow yourself to dream big and then move forward by setting goals.

You will find motivation and inspiration when you set goals and have something to work toward - a purpose greater than yourself. Find something that inspires you to get out of bed in the morning and look ahead. Never look back; the past will cause your eyes to focus in the wrong direction. Instead, make the choice to focus forward so you can move into a place of peace and excitement.

> *"For I know the plans I have for you,"* declares the Lord, *"plans to prosper you and not to harm you, plans to give you hope and a future."*
> *Jeremiah 29:11*

I encourage you to take some time to reflect inward and search for your gifts. Here are some questions to get you started.

1. What did you enjoy doing as a child?
2. What makes your heart race with excitement?
3. What are your hobbies?
4. Ask your close family members and friends what they see as your gifts and strengths.
5. What do you do in your pastime, in the evenings, on the weekends?

Do you have a gift for pottery, music, teaching, counseling? Do you like solitude or being around others? Sometimes, due to the busyness of life, current job demands, family demands or past experiences, these are hard to identify. You've been working for someone else for so long or doing what you were "supposed" to do that you've lost sight of the gifts you've been given. We start to think that everyone is good at "that" when, in reality, everyone is not. Because our gift comes easy to us, we tend to think that it comes easy for everyone. This is a great misconception. What comes easy to you may be totally unthinkable for others.

For example, my father loves working on cars. As I write this book I know he is working on restoring a Corvette. He's been working on it for at least four months, every day. This is one of his gifts and he is passionate about it. I, on the other hand, couldn't tell you a thing about a car's makeup except if I think the paint color is pretty. Growing up my father taught me how to change the oil in my car and learn basic car "things." Sorry, Dad, I take my car to the dealer now because this is not my gift or where any of my passion lies.

> *We have different gifts, according to the grace given us. If a man's gift is prophesying, let him use it in proportion to his faith. If it is serving, let him serve; if it is teaching, let him teach; if it is encouraging, let him encourage; if it is contributing to the needs of others, let him give generously; if it is leadership, let him govern diligently; if it is showing mercy, let him do it cheerfully.*
> **Romans 12:6-8**

Never doubt that you were designed with specific gifts and it is up to you to step out into God's greatness and use those gifts. It is not only good for you, but for the greater good of others. There is only one YOU that can fulfill the calling God has for YOU.

I have realized that the better I know myself, the more in control my life becomes. Remember, you are the driver of your life and the better you know yourself, including your gifts and abilities, the more direct your road will be in achieving greatness.

Romans 8:31b says, "If God is for us, who can be against us?" What a bold, inspiring and fearless statement! During my time of reflection and grieving I repeated this scripture over and over and over. God is on our side; He wants the best for us. And if He is on our side, who dare be against us! Repeating this gave me confidence and courage to move on with certainty that God has a life full of blessings waiting for each of us. We have a ginormous God - not a God who wants mediocrity!

> *I have learned that success is to be measured not so much by the position that one has reached in life as by the obstacles which he has overcome while trying to succeed.*
> **Booker T. Washington**

I don't know your specific loss or where you may be at this particular time in your life, but I do know that God is for us and is on our side cheering for us. He wants to use the difficulties in our lives for greater good. Maybe our character is being shaped to help someone else down the road or we're being guided into a new, better path. I don't know your loss but I do know that there is hope and a bright future that lies ahead for you.

Chapter 3

What Is Your Ginormous Goal?

Webster's dictionary defines a goal as the end toward which effort is directed.
Albert Einstein defined insanity as doing the same thing over and over again and expecting different results. If you can relate to this, now's the time to make a shift into a season of abundance.

One of my goals was to run a marathon, all 26.2 miles of it! In order to achieve it, I had to want it badly enough to make it a goal. Lord knows committing to this goal made my knees shake with fear and doubt. Many of my family members and friends thought I was crazy. Once I made up my mind that it was, in fact, my goal, I made my plan. I joined a local running group and began training. I couldn't just wake up one morning and decide to run 26.2 miles; I had to train. I trained for six months - six very long months. Along the way I met some of the most wonderful women. We trained together, laughed together, cried together and accomplished the goal of finishing the marathon together. Let me just say that who you "run" with in life is critical. Don't hang with energy suckers. I'll talk more about this later.

I don't want to sugar-coat this goal because it was not easy for me! I had just started getting back into running so I was only running about two miles, maybe three times a week. I knew nothing about running a distance that seemed to start from Dallas and end in Egypt, but I was willing to learn. There were many days when I didn't feel like setting the alarm clock to get out of my nice, warm, cozy bed at 4:30 a.m. Every night I had to lay my running clothes out so it was a little easier to hit the alarm button, roll out of bed, into my clothes and out the door.

One of my trainers used to say that the hardest part of training for a marathon is putting your shoes on and getting out the door. Every single morning I had to tell myself, "Just put your shoes on and get out the door." Some days were incredibly hot, some days it rained and other days I was so sore from the prior day's run that I could barely put one foot in front of the other, but I did. I had to remind myself every morning why I was doing this and my "why" had to be greater than any obstacles. My "why" was to prove to myself that my body could push beyond my expectations.

Accomplishing this goal gave me the confidence to move forward and set more goals - loftier goals. So lofty that I decided to train for a second marathon in an effort to qualify for the Boston Marathon. What was I thinking?

My second marathon was not nearly as pleasant as my first marathon. I followed the same steps as far as setting my goal, training and nutrition. However, during the

WHAT IS YOUR GINORMOUS GOAL?

marathon at about mile 13, I wanted to hop on the back of that motorcycle escort and call it a day. My EVERYTHING hurt! I finished the marathon but it was a completely different experience. Why? It was the same 26.2 miles, same training, same nutrition plan and same camaraderie. What changed? What changed was the six inches between my ears. The weather was cold and windy, my girlfriends and I got separated at mile 13 and I was trying to qualify for the Boston Marathon which meant shaving 19 minutes off of my first marathon finish time.

My mindset changed, negativity set in and I began to doubt myself. I learned much more from my challenging second marathon than I had from my first. It taught me that setting goals begins in our mind and requires adherence. To be clear, goal-setting is not easy. Only eight percent of the general population can identify clear goals, and only about three percent ever actually write those goals down.[2] Each goal is different, with different expectations, different outcomes, different circumstances. It is how you deal with changes along the way that will set you apart. As Laurence Johnson Peter wrote, "If you don't know where you are going, you will probably end up somewhere else."

Living with purpose is how we are designed; being specific and purposeful each day in the decisions we make is a choice, our choice.

Let's take a deeper look into goal setting. Now that you've taken time to truly understand your gifts, what's the next step? The next step is to define your goals and get SMART. Zig Ziglar wrote, "With definite goals you release your own power, and things start happening." Your goals can be anything from financial, physical, or spiritual to career, family, or personal development. Having a plan of action is your first step.

> *May he give you the desire of your heart and make all your plans succeed. We will shout for joy when you are victorious and will lift up our banners in the name of our God. May the Lord grant all your requests.*
> *Psalm 20:4-5*

There are five steps in defining your SMART goals.

1. Specific – Be specific.
2. Measurable – Make it measurable.
3. Actionable – Define your plan of action.
4. Reach – Set your sights high and reach.
5. Timeline – Set a defined timeline.

Someone once said, plan your work then work your plan. If you take the time to be SMART with your goals, working your plan becomes a step-by-step guide to follow. Before you know it you're accomplishing ginormous goals one step at a time!

==The first step is to define your goal.== I am a big believer in list making, so I've created a template to use as your goal sheet. This SMART goal sheet can be used for the smallest to the loftiest of goals. Some of you may have a goal to get up every day at a certain time, to work out twice a week, to cut out coffee from your daily diet, to spend more quality time with your family, to eat healthy, to pay off a debt, to build an authentic friendship with someone, or to limit your shopping. I don't know your goals but I do know that this goal sheet makes your goals intentional; therefore, I know you will succeed. To help get you started, there are blank goal sheets in the back of this book.

For example, my husband Ron and I started listening to and reading books from the financial guru, author and Nationally Syndicated Radio Host, Dave Ramsey. After listening to his straight forward talk about having financial peace, we decided to set a lofty goal to pay off all our debt. How lofty was it? Well, Ron and I just got married and had paid for our wedding, we remodeled Ron's former bachelor pad from floors to ceilings, plus my student loan was still staring at us. These endeavors left us with a lot of debt. Talk about reaching high and praying boldly on this goal! It certainly left me feeling a little sick to my stomach. This was a lot of money for us.

So how did we achieve our goal? We completed a SMART goal sheet and stuck with it. In fact, I've shared part of it below *(the numbers used are only an example)*. I hope our family's example provides you with the insight, optimism and confidence needed to achieve whatever you set your mind to.

SMART GOAL TEMPLATE	
MY GOAL IS:	
To pay off all $5,000 of debt, except the home mortgage.	
SPECIFIC:	
To pay off in order from smallest to largest:	
Credit Card #1	$200
Home Depot Credit Card	$500
Credit Card #2	$1,200
Student Loan	$1,300
Credit Card #3	$1,800
Grand Total	**$5,000**
MEASURABLE:	
Every two weeks sit down together and review the budget and debt payoff plan.	
Are we eliminating debt every month?	
Are we debt free one year after beginning the plan?	
Are we on track? Do we need to make any adjustments?	
ACTION PLAN:	
Create a written monthly budget to track every dollar spent.	
REACH HIGH:	
Yes, it makes me a little nauseous!!!	
TIMELINE:	
Review written budget every two weeks.	
Begin debt payoff March 6, 2009.	
Accomplish goal March 6, 2010.	

God blessed our family tremendously and we were able to not only pay off the debt, but pay it off three months early. We were so inspired by paying off our debt that we decided to reward others along the way. Each time we paid off a debt, we gave $25 to someone in need. Our next goal? To pay off our home mortgage. How? With our SMART goal sheet!

Creating a goal sheet helps you to stay focused and live on purpose. Every thought and every decision is based on your goals. This makes your decision-making process much easier. When you're facing a decision all you have to do is ask yourself one simple question, "Does this help support or detract from my goal?" If it supports your goal, proceed. You are now living with intention!

Accomplishing your goals may not be easy but I guarantee you that the things you work hardest to achieve will bring you the biggest sense of accomplishment and satisfaction.

Beware that not all your family and friends will understand or support your goals. You must remain focused and believe that you can accomplish ginormous goals. When Ron and I set some of our goals we had to make sacrifices and I'm sure there were people who thought we were crazy. Sometimes *we* thought we were crazy! To others our sacrifices may have appeared extreme, weird and over-the-top different; but in the end, different paid off and we are now living debt-free as a result of hard work, discipline and clear focus. You, too, can accomplish goals that will change the trajectory of your life and the lives of others around you for generations to come!

No matter how big or how small you think your goal is, the size does not matter. What matters is that you're building a new, healthy habit of living on purpose with clear intention of where you're going and when. This is the most important lesson that I can convey to you in this chapter.

There have been times when I've set a lofty goal but didn't achieve that goal when I had planned. Sometimes I fall short, circumstances change and I have to adjust my plan and my attitude. Let me be clear: This is not failure! Just make the adjustments needed and stick with your enhanced plan. Again, you plan your work and work your plan.

In the book *How to Be Like Women of Influence*, one of the common characteristics that each of the 20 women possessed was goal setting. Each one of the women featured, from Oprah Winfrey to Mother Teresa to Helen Keller to Rosa Parks, set ginormous goals related to the unique gifts with which they were created. Once they set their specific goals they worked toward accomplishing those goals.

> *Be persistent in pursuing your dreams.*
> *Oprah Winfrey*

I believe with every fiber of my being that setting ginormous goals breathes life and vitality into our souls. Do you have something to look at every day to keep you on track, to think big, to pray boldly and inspire you? Having something to visualize daily will help keep you motivated.

Having a vision board or goal poster with your goal sheets and photos is a daily inspiration that will keep you

WHAT IS YOUR GINORMOUS GOAL?

excited and on track to achieve your success. I create a new vision board every year with my new goals and I place it where I will see it every day - usually the kitchen because I love food. This vision provides direction, peace and a constant reminder that God has so much more in store for each of us than we can imagine. It is said that energy goes where attention flows. So let's focus our attention on the positives in our lives and our ginormous goals! Remember, all things begin in our mind. If we think positive thoughts, positive results will follow.

The opposite also is true, so be very careful of what you allow into your mind and where you choose to dwell. This means being cautious with the television programs we watch, the radio stations we listen to and the people we run with. Garbage in, garbage out; ginormous goals in, ginormous goals out.

As you think about your goals, think big, pray boldly and put pen to paper. For my vision board/goal poster I use a piece of poster board, old magazines and whatever else I can find that will reinforce my goals. I also have my SMART goal sheet attached so I can check my progress every day. As the saying goes, "Whatever the mind can conceive and believe you can achieve." So reach high and stay with it!

Additional tools to keep you on track with your goals are daily affirmations and a "top five" list. My daily affirmations come from everywhere! Whenever I read a good quote or a scripture that is relevant to a specific season in my life, I write it down or cut it out and place it around my house. In the back of this book I have included some of my favorite quotes that you may tear out and place around your house for daily inspiration.

I also create a daily "top five" list that keeps me focused on my goals. This daily list keeps me living with intention. Here is an example of my "top five" list for today:

1. Work on book for at least three hours.
2. Make one contact with a book publisher/editor.
3. Research articles for at least one hour.
4. Exercise for 40 minutes.
5. Work on profile book with Ron.

I keep this list with me and I glance at it often. When I accomplish an item I cross it off the list. There is something that happens mentally when you cross an item off the list. It marks the accomplishment of a small win and how you're living with purpose. I tested this "top five" list with hundreds of people throughout my corporate career and in researching to write this book. This is what a few people had to say.

- ✓ I feel more productive.
- ✓ A list provides focus for the day.
- ✓ Writing a list of only five things makes me think through what's most important to me.
- ✓ I love the feeling of crossing things off my list. Sometimes I add tasks to my list just so I can cross them off! Is that cheating?
- ✓ Some days when I don't feel like I'm accomplishing anything I can look back at my list and realize that I have accomplished at least a few

things. That makes me happy and urges me to keep moving.
- ✓ My husband and I make our lists every night and compare the next day who finished all five things the quickest. It adds a little healthy competition.
- ✓ The list adds an element of accountability.

Once you've identified your goals, detailed your SMART goal sheet and created visual reminders, share your goals with others. Sharing your goals out loud will create accountability, but most important, it builds your confidence and creates a network of encouragers. Share your ginormous goals with people who will encourage you, cheer for you at each milestone of accomplishment and get excited with and for you.

At this point you have your ginormous goal(s) and a few tools to keep you on track. Now let's look at outrageous enthusiasm that will sustain you in times of trial and doubt. As an old Chinese proverb states, "The longest journey begins with a single step." Let's step into the next chapter and look at having outrageous enthusiasm.

Chapter 4

Outrageous Enthusiasm!

Ralph Waldo Emerson said, "Nothing great was ever achieved without enthusiasm."

Congratulations to you! I want to encourage you to continue on this journey of exploring your Ginormous, Outrageous, Audacious Life! You're working through your loss, you've refocused your energy to realize the gifts God has designed for you and you've set goals based on these gifts. My hope is that you're excited to move toward achieving the greatness that is waiting for you.

The word enthusiasm comes from a Greek word meaning "God within."

Scripture says that no person has ever seen, heard, or imagined the wonderful things He has in store. That's right; God wants us to live up to our full potential, no settling. His desires for each of us are bigger than we could ever dream or imagine. I see it so often where we get comfortable and begin to believe that getting through the week is an acceptable way of life. We see this reflected everywhere in marketing efforts: TGIF, Working for the Weekend and many other clichés.

I believe we are to live every day with outrageous enthusiasm. We only get this one set of 24 hours; let's make the most of it. I don't ever want to live a life full of regrets or what ifs. I envision arriving at the pearly white gates, looking at our Father and hearing the words, "Well done, good and faithful servant." I don't want to have to explain why I chose the path of least resistance because I was comfortable or afraid. The beautiful thing is that each day is a new beginning. Each day we have a choice of what we will do with these 24 hours, and if we will live with outrageous enthusiasm. Each day is a fresh start. Yesterday is behind us so don't focus on what was or what should've been; refocus on what you want today - what can be.

> *If you have any encouragement from being united with Christ, if any comfort from his love, if any fellowship with the Spirit, if any tenderness and compassion, then make my joy complete by being like-minded, having the same love, being one in spirit and purpose. Do nothing out of selfish ambition or vain conceit, but in humility consider others better than yourselves. Each of you should look not only to your own interests, but also to the interests of others. Your attitude should be the same as that of Christ Jesus.*
>   *Philippians 2:1-5*

OUTRAGEOUS ENTHUSIASM!

There are days when we wake up and don't feel enthusiastic. Believe me, this morning was one of those days for me. The alarm went off and I wanted to pull the covers over my head and go back to sleep. It took me a few moments but I got up, spent an hour reading and praying, went for a run and am now ready to start my day enthusiastically. It was a choice. I could've stayed in bed and "got through" the day merely fulfilling these next 24 hours but I had to make the choice to make the most of this day. In the big picture we have just a few moments on this earth and it is up to us each and every day to choose to live with enthusiasm in our hearts.

> *Life is a mirror and will reflect back to the thinker what he thinks into it.*
> ***Ernest Holmes***

Some days are more of a choice than others, like those days the house needs cleaning. From my viewpoint house cleaning is one of those necessary evils. I don't think anyone ever thinks: "Yay, I get to clean the house today!" It's usually more along the lines of, "Hmmmmm, I have to clean the house today." My house cleaning ritual begins with putting on some great dance music, as loud as I can stand it. Then I begin dancing while grabbing the vacuum cleaner. It's amazing what a great dance partner the vacuum cleaner can be. After about five minutes, I start feeling enthusiastic. It begins in the mind, and soon my entire household gets involved, including my seven-pound Bichon Frise and 70-pound Black Lab. This may be a small, even trivial, activity but it demonstrates the power of enthusiasm. My house gets cleaned and all three of us have fun.

Have you ever noticed that enthusiasm is contagious? Think about a great pair of shoes that you've purchased, a good book you've read or a recent movie you've seen. Didn't you tell everybody about it? Soon all of your family and friends have seen that movie, read that book or gone to that same store to look for shoes. It's because of your enthusiasm - it was contagious!

> *A cheerful heart is good medicine, but a crushed spirit dries up the bones.*
> **Proverbs 17:22**

This concept is so important because you will run into obstacles along the way to your great successes and without enthusiasm you are much more apt to throw in the towel. I know it can be difficult, but God's confidence in you greatly outweighs any negative thoughts that you may encounter. I know that you can achieve your goals, and isn't it much more fun doing it with outrageous enthusiasm? What you think about you bring about!

You are what you think about; therefore, if you focus on the positives in your life and are enthusiastic, you will experience positive results.

My friend Beth is a great example of having outrageous enthusiasm. Almost two years ago a seed was planted in Beth to begin her own marketing firm, specializing in the hospitality industry. Although this seed had been planted in the back of her mind, she didn't know how, when or if this dream was to come to fruition.

She diligently prayed about this dream and we walked many, many miles discussing the pros and cons of beginning her business. Finally the day presented itself to Beth and she embarked on this journey and dream of beginning her own marketing firm.

While she quickly learned about running a business, from accounting practices to technical support to legalities and taxes, she consistently possessed an outrageously enthusiastic attitude. During a time where Beth could've let fear and doubt overpower her thoughts, she decided daily to live with outrageous enthusiasm.

I'm happy to share with you that Beth's business is thriving in a time where the economy has taken a huge hit. Someone must've forgotten to tell her about the downturn of the economy, especially in the hospitality industry. This is the power of possessing outrageous enthusiasm.

We must make our intentions clear, state it and claim it. Our thoughts and enthusiasm truly determine our future. We are the drivers of our own success.

> *The thief comes only to steal and kill and destroy; I have come that they may have life, and have it to the full.*
> *John 10:10*

Another key factor to help you live with an outrageously enthusiastic attitude is giving back, random acts of kindness or paying it forward. I will talk about this further in a later chapter but it is so important that I want to mention it here since it can be influential to your attitude. When we take the focus off of ourselves and put it onto someone else it creates excitement within our soul.

Never underestimate the power of you! If you don't believe me try this activity over the next four weeks and you'll be truly amazed. It doesn't take a lot of time but it makes all the difference.

1. Find one positive characteristic about yourself every day. Below are just a few examples to help you get started.

    a. Your smile.

    b. Your sense of humor.

    c. You solved a problem at home or at work.

    d. You worked out today.

    e. You had a great hair day.

    f. You had a productive day.

    g. You lived today enthusiastically.

    h. You made a top five list today.

2. Conduct one random act of kindness each day. Below are some examples. Remember this does not have to involve money.

    a. Make someone laugh.

    b. Give someone a hug.

    c. Point out someone's God-given gifts.

    d. Be patient with your spouse/children.

OUTRAGEOUS ENTHUSIASM!

    e. While at the restaurant or coffee shop drive thru, pay for the car behind you.

    f. Visit an assisted living facility and brighten one person's day.

    g. Mow a neighbor's lawn.

    h. Take dinner to someone in need.

3. Find or write a quote of inspiration and place it where you'll see it every day. Repeat this quote at least once a day, every day over the next four weeks.

I believe that at the end of your four weeks you will have formed enthusiasm as a new habit. Aristotle said, "We are what we repeatedly do. Excellence, then, is not an act, but a habit."

Before I end this chapter let me share with you a personal story on how outrageous enthusiasm truly works.

One beautiful, sunny Dallas day my friend Beth and I went to a local lake to take a casual walk before heading to breakfast. Beth had on a cute pair of Capri pants, a tank top and flip flops. I had on a pair of running shorts, a running top and running shoes. After about 45 minutes into our walk Beth was ready to head back to the car. Well, with my outrageous enthusiasm I convinced her that we were already half way around the lake so we should just keep walking. It was a gorgeous day, we were having great conversation and I thought a little further wouldn't hurt. Because of my outrageous enthusiasm Beth agreed to continue our walk. Do you remember that Beth had on flip flops?

Needless to say, nine miles later, in flip flops, her enthusiasm was wearing off. After the blisters healed and soreness dissipated we decided that we probably shouldn't do that again! But you can see the power of enthusiasm, which will be remembered far longer than the pain of a few blisters.

Outrageous enthusiasm has power greater than we will ever fully realize so let's give it a try and experience some fantastic results.

Chapter 5
Audacious: Overcoming Fear and Intimidation

> *There is no fear in love. But perfect love drives out fear, because fear has to do with punishment. The one who fears is not made perfect in love.*
> *1 John 4:18*

In part, the definition of audacious means invulnerable to fear or intimidation.

Fear can minimize your life. Fear can be paralyzing, it can thwart God's plans for you and, more important, it will eat away at your soul.

Fear is a funny thing. I seem to remember fearful times more than most other memories. I remember when I was a little girl learning how to ride a bike, how fearful I was to get rid of those training wheels. One day my father decided that it was time. He removed the training wheels, placed me on the bike (which was sitting on a hill), and gave me a push. I made it five or six feet and fell over. After falling I realized that was probably the worst it could get. While still fearful about falling, I decided to get back on the bike and try again.

The point is that we must continue to work through the fears and intimidation because if we don't, it will rob us of the greatest gifts God has for us. We must not live in fear but in confidence that God's got our back. When we let fear overcome us we allow the devil to steal our peace, joy, growth and purpose.

You can conquer almost any fear if you will only make up your mind to do so. For remember, fear doesn't exist anywhere except in the mind.
    Dale Carnegie

Fear defeats more people than any other one thing in the world.
    Ralph Waldo Emerson

When I was in university I was a member of the

Wisconsin State Action Team for the Wisconsin Marketing and Management Association. As a member of the State Action Team, you had to be elected to one of eight positions to represent your region within the state. I was not fearful during the campaign; I just followed the advice of a few great professors and mentors. I was thrilled to be voted into this role and begin my one-year term.

One of the responsibilities of this role was to host conferences which included a great deal of public speaking. I was 19 years young at the time and didn't have a lot of public speaking experience. One of the first conferences I was involved in hosting included over 500 attendees. Talk about fear; palms sweating, butterflies in my stomach, things shaking that should not be shaking! Shaking so much that one of my fellow female state officers and I used to joke and call it the "rump shaker." I can remember those feelings even as I write these words. Years later I still remember those conferences and the fear, but now I can laugh about those "opportunities for growth."

God used that period to shape and mold me. I later went into a position in corporate America where I had several large public speaking events every month. I'm so thankful for the early "rump-shaking" days when I learned how to overcome fear and be an encourager who would help others achieve their ginormous goals.

If we allow our fears to rule our lives we also allow it to determine how high we rise. Sometimes you don't realize that God is working behind the scenes and He is using you to light the way for so many others. To live up to our full potential we must overcome fears, insecurities and intimidation.

> *You gain strength, courage and confidence by every experience in which you really stop to look fear in the face. You must do the thing which you think you cannot do.*
> **Eleanor Roosevelt**

I once heard someone explain fear as False Evidence Appearing Real. I love this explanation because it reminds me that, more times than not, we fear the unfound, unknown and untold. After all, what is the worst that could happen - a fall on a bike, a little "rump shaking"? How much stronger we become when we chose to work through the fear and break into a place of confidence, peace and joy.

I wonder how many times we allow fear to overshadow God's desires for our lives? One day over coffee and great conversation, my friend Sharon asked me a profound question: "How many little miracles do we miss every day?" If we just got out of our own way, how many more opportunities and miracles would we experience? Sometimes we allow our past filters, failures and faults to determine our future.

> *Anybody who believes in something without reservation believes that this thing is right and should be, has the stamina to meet obstacles and overcome them.*
> **Golda Meir**

> *"I took you from the ends of the earth, from its farthest corners I called you. I said, 'You are my servant'; I have chosen you and have not rejected you. So do not fear, for I am with you; do not be dismayed, for I am your God. I will strengthen you and help you; I will uphold you with my righteous right hand."*
> **Isaiah 41:9-10**

What comforting words. We all face fears; the key is to move through the fear to experience the excellence waiting for us on the other side.

Clara Barton was known for her determination, she simply said, "Dare to do."

It has become tradition for my friend Beth and I to celebrate birthdays together. We've been doing this for almost 10 years. What began as a simple birthday dinner has evolved into a birthday weekend where our husbands must get clearance on any birthday plans they may have in order to avoid any conflict with the girls birthday weekend plans. Some of these birthday weekends have included weekend spa retreats, trips out of town, shopping; but, most important, it is just a few days of great conversation, good food and lots of laughter.

One year Beth took me to a spa retreat where we had the opportunity to experience first-hand the art of trapeze. We both were very excited *until* we had to climb up a teeny tiny ladder for two stories and stand on a platform that was barely wide enough for both feet to fit on! But that was only the beginning. As a trapeze performer, you must grab the bar, swing upside down with your knees locked around the bar and fling your body forward into some stranger called "the catcher," hoping that he'll catch you. This was not one of my finer moments, nor was it a pretty sight! Imagine: We're in Texas, it's hot, and I'm standing on the platform two stories above the ground strapped into a harness that, in my opinion, resembled a diaper. Finally in place, the instructor yells for me to fall forward off of the platform and swing on the bar. I was so full of fear that I could barely breathe let alone jump. I had a choice to make, I could either crawl back down this teeny tiny ladder to safe ground or I could choose to face my fear and fall forward.

I decided to face my fear and fall forward. What a feeling! I felt like I was flying! But now the instructor was yelling at me to let go of the bar - what?!? The instructor yelled up to me, "Let go!" I continued swinging with my hands fully embracing the bar. I couldn't let go. He yelled again, "Let go of the bar!" Again I continued squeezing the bar as tight as my white knuckles would allow. After what seemed like eternity and much convincing from the instructor that I was safe, I let go of the bar and flung myself towards the "catcher" man. I didn't even come close to the "catcher" man. I did an all-out belly flop right into the net that was waiting for me below.

That weekend, I learned so many things about myself and overcoming my fears. Although I must confess, I have never been more excited to get my two feet back on solid ground.

Another important lesson to learn is that we are not alone in the area of fear. Working through our fears may not look pretty, as my trapeze experience clearly demonstrated; however, we must make the bold decision to move through the fear to prevent the fear from defining us.

Just as the trapeze instructor could see the whole picture, while I could only see a teeny tiny ladder, a sorry looking platform and some sagging net, God sees the whole picture. He guides us through our fears with His best in mind. Our faith in Him will get us there, even when we can't see the bigger picture.

Some of the most successful people in our history worked through their own fears, falling forward into success. I can't imagine how different this world would be without some of our most historical figures pushing through their fears to bring innovation and creativity to the forefront.

Falling Forward

1. Bill Gates, Co-Founder, Chairman and Chief Software and Architect of the world's largest software firm, Microsoft Corporation, dropped out of college.

2. Steve Jobs, Apple Computers, was stripped of his duties with Apple in 1985. Later he was asked to rejoin the company.

3. Walt Disney, Walt Disney Company, was told that he was not creative enough and failed at several start-up companies.

4. Michael Dell, Dell Inc., received average grades in high school, dropped out of college and was told that he'd never get anywhere.

5. Donald Trump failed in early investments which resulted in bankruptcy.

6. Albert Einstein had speech difficulty as a child to such an extent that his parents thought he was mentally challenged. He also failed his university entrance exam.
7. Winston Churchill failed the sixth grade.
8. Michael Bloomberg, Larry King and Oprah Winfrey were all fired from prior jobs.

These people pushed through their fears and have accomplished audacious living!

Many times the only way we learn is the hard way. We remember these lessons and hopefully we pick ourselves up, dust off our knees and fall forward with more wisdom and knowledge. It takes courage, belief and persistence to overcome fear. The more you face your fears, the more you grow and the stronger you stand.

If the Lord delights in a man's way, he makes his steps firm; though he stumble, he will not fall, for the Lord upholds him with his hand.
Psalm 37:23-24

Chapter 6
Living in a Circle of Influence

Having a positive, encouraging and supportive circle of influence is a major contribution to your success. Having friends and family in your circle of influence that will encourage you when you're down and praise you to success is so important to your health, both physically and mentally.

Think of a time when you've experienced a difficult situation. Did you have someone to talk with honestly and openly about the situation? Did you walk away feeling lifted up or beaten down? This will help you determine a healthy circle of influence. A healthy circle of family and friends love you in good times, bad times, beautiful times and flat-out ugly times.

> *A friend loves at all times, and a brother is born for adversity.*
> ***Proverbs 17:17***

I've been blessed throughout my life with wonderful friendships. These friends have molded me into who I am today through their love, honesty and support.

Several years ago I had a work trip held in Maui, Hawaii, where my cousin Beth joined me after my work commitment. While there we decided that we wanted to step outside our comfort zone and try a few new activities.

One of the activities we looked forward to was riding a bike for more than 30 miles down Mount Haleakala. Mount Haleakala rises over 10,000 feet (3,000 meters) above sea level and is known for its unique scenery. After reading that Mark Twain visited this dormant volcano in 1866 and wrote that this was "the most sublime spectacle I ever witnessed and the memory of it will remain with me always," I had to experience it up close and personal. In order to watch the sun rise, the tour began at 2 a.m. Once my alarm clock went off and I finally realized that the horrible sound was not a fire alarm but from something I had actually set, we quickly got up and walked down to the designated meeting spot and greeted our tour guide.

There were roughly 30-40 people in our group who were all about as awake as we were. Soon after we arrived, we experienced the most amazing sunrise that we have ever seen. Beth and I, in a state of serenity, stood in awe of the peaceful beauty. Shortly after viewing this very tranquil sunrise our tour guide began explaining the biking guidelines for the ride. I must admit that neither of us were paying attention to our tour guide because we were still in our very peaceful, tranquil place.

As our tour guide continued talking we started coming back to reality and actually perked up as he mentioned something about accidents, bike crashes, out of control people, ambulances and blood. Our sudden alertness quickly moved into shock as the realization sunk in that we may have just signed up for something similar to bumper cars or roller derby on bikes. Then our guide handed us a questionable contraption that he called a bike. By this time, we had both left our peaceful, tranquil place far, far behind. The tour guide finished his speech and then called us in order of the lineup. God has a sense of humor because the very first name that the tour guide called was Beth's. Not only had we not been paying attention, but now she was leading the pack. (Keep in mind that neither of us had been on a bike since grade school.)

As my cousin made her way to the number one position I thought to myself, "If this isn't stepping outside our comfort zone I don't know what is!"

The best way to describe our first several pedals is, Weebles wobbles! If it wasn't for Beth's outrageous enthusiasm to complete this activity I assure you that I would still have been sound asleep in my hotel room.

Our group pulled out with Beth leading the pack. The first few miles were a little rough; however, Beth had the courage to take charge and lead our group down this 30 mile tour. She let the road guide her and the rest of us followed.

The bike ride turned out to be the highlight of the trip and one that I always will cherish. If it wasn't for her encouragement and extra push I may have missed this once-in-a-lifetime experience. This is the power of having a strong circle of influence.

> *Grief can take care of itself, but to get the full value of a joy you must have somebody to divide it with.*
> *Mark Twain*

The people who make up your circle of influence push you in a healthy way to accomplish and achieve more than you ever thought possible. These people know, support and encourage your ginormous goals; they offer outrageous enthusiasm at the perfect time, at the perfect place and with the perfect heart.

This group of people helps you overcome fears and challenges and they are with you to experience the highs and lows that life can bring. These types of friends serve as my "board of directors" and influence my life decisions.

Do you have a circle of influence? Do you have people who inspire you to be your best and maximize the gifts you have? Do you have people that breathe belief into you? It is so important to surround yourself with friends who are positive thinkers and not energy suckers.

Energy suckers are those who complain constantly, live in drama and want you to ride with them on a roundabout road. This road is a never-ending circle that never moves forward. A conversation with an energy sucker leaves you feeling worn out. I'm not saying to eliminate these people altogether from your life, I'm only suggesting that you consider the amount of time that you spend with them.

> *One loyal friend is worth ten thousand relatives.*
> *Euripides, Greek playwrite*

I have three categories within my circle of influence.

1. **Sprinters**
2. **Marathoners**
3. **Inner Circle**

The sprinters are the largest group of people. These are friends I see once in awhile. It's good to see them and catch up but they may come for only a season. These friendships may be more short distance or surface level. I don't share deep, intimate details with this group. It's more of a fun, light-hearted, conversational group of friends. These friends are wonderful and I love each and every one of them.

The next group of friends are those who I call marathoners. These are the friends that I've had for years. We've grown up together; they know my family and have been with me through many seasons or marathons. I see these friends maybe once a month or maybe even once every few months. No matter how long between visits, we always pick up right where we left off from our last conversation. These friends are true gems. I trust these wonderful friends and I cherish them dearly.

This last group is my inner circle. I can count on one hand the number of people in my inner circle. This group knows everything about me from my greatest achievements to my most embarrassing moments and deepest secrets. This group of friends is there for me if I call at two in the afternoon or two in the morning. This magnificent group of women love me unconditionally and whole-heartedly.

We encourage each other, we are 100% honest with each other, even when it's difficult to say or receive. We bring out the best in each other and I adore, respect and would give my life for each and every one of these spectacular women. These women and their friendships remind me a lot of David and Jonathan's relationship from the Bible.

After David had finished talking with Saul, Jonathan became one in spirit with David, and he loved him as himself. From that day Saul kept David with him and did not let him return to his father's house. And Jonathan made a covenant with David because he loved him as himself. Jonathan took off the robe he was wearing and gave it to David, along with his tunic, and even his sword, his bow and his belt.
1 Samuel 18:1-4

LIVING IN A CIRCLE OF INFLUENCE

Just as with my inner circle friends, the love and friendship between these two men could not be broken even in the toughest of times. It is said that loyalty is one of life's most costly qualities, that it is the most selfless part of love. Do you surround yourself with these types of friends? This level of friendship is rare. Some of us may only find this type of friendship once in an entire lifetime. I consider it a true blessing to have such an influential, powerful and courageous group of inner circle friends. I don't take these friends for granted and I try very hard to protect these relationships. I can say that I run with a remarkable group of women who have hearts of gold, minds of brilliance and personalities of authenticity.

Who do you "run" with? Think about the people in your life that you spend the most time with and ask yourself the following questions.

1. Do your friends encourage you to step outside your comfort zone?

2. Are your friends positive and do they encourage you to reach your goals?

3. Do they breathe belief into you?

4. Are they loyal to you in both the wonderful times and the challenging times of your life?

5. Do they offer wise council?

6. Are they 100% honest with you even if they know it may be a difficult conversation?

7. Do they love you unconditionally?

It is important to have a healthy mix of sprinters, marathoners and inner circle friends. Just be cautious of where you're spending the majority of your time. Positive minds accomplish positive results.

> *He who walks with the wise grows wise, but a companion of fools suffers harm.*
> *Proverbs 13:20*

Who you surround yourself with influences the trajectory of your life. If you want to become more patient, you may want to find and run with patient people. If you want to become debt free, find some debt-free people and run with them. If you want to begin your own business, find some role model business leaders and run with them. What you allow into your body, mind and soul plants seeds that will sprout. You reap what you sow.

Oprah Winfrey has three key philosophies about living in a circle of influence.

1. Get rid of the backstabbers. Surround yourself only with people who will lift you higher.

2. Surround yourself with people who are as smart, or smarter than, you.

3. When people show you who they are, believe them the first time.

It's a blessing to have a lot of friends, just be cautious that your inner circle aligns with your priorities.

> *True happiness consists not in the multitude of friends, but in their worth and choice.*
> **Samuel Johnston, British lexicographer**

Several months ago, I began a Bible study that has transformed into amazing friendships. These women come every week honestly, humbly and courageously. We come together to study God's word but also because we truly love and care about each other. God has blessed this group of women with beautiful bonds that will last a lifetime. My intention of forming this Bible study was for us to continue learning God's word, but God had so much more in store for all of us. He had inner circle connections in store for us.

Two weeks ago one of the women from our Bible study, Susan, arrived for our weekly study but was very quiet. If you knew our sweet friend Susan you would know that she is anything but quiet. Towards the end of the evening she expressed anxiety for finding a home for her parents within a certain location, within a certain price range and within a very tight timeframe. The stress of this was building upon her shoulders and it was physically and mentally taking a toll on her. That evening we prayed for her. Our group believes in praying boldly so we weren't just asking God to find her parents any house; we had specific requests. We prayed that God would bring a house to Susan and her parents that was close to the rest of the family; we prayed that the house would honor her parents since they've spent a lifetime helping others in need; and we prayed that it was financially reasonable. Lastly, we prayed that God would deliver the house fast!

Through this stressful time we were all able to encourage Susan and pray for her. We took time to reflect on God's goodness and His complete control of every situation, of every detail and of His perfect timing. We stood together united in deep friendship, cheering on our dear friend Susan as the search continued.

No joke, as I sat typing this chapter, my phone rang and it was Susan. She called to tell me that she found the perfect house, in the perfect location, at the perfect price range and in the perfect timeframe. Within one week they closed on this perfect house. Today we get to celebrate with her! It pays to have an inner circle with the same core values, praying together, to be each other's encouragers, to be honest with each other and to push each other to reach the full potential that God has in store for us.

Susan is now helping her parents move into their dream house.

I share this story with you because I want these types of authentic friendships for you. I want you to experience the absolute best that God has in store for you. My hope is that you run with people who dream big, pray bold and love deep. This truly is the sweet spot of life.

Thus nature has no love for solitude, and always leans, as it were, on some support; and the sweetest support is found in the most intimate friendship.
   Cicero

Associate yourself with men of good quality if you esteem your own reputation; for 'tis better to be alone than in bad company."
  George Washington

My friends are my estate.
  Emily Dickinson

True friendship is a plant of slow growth, and must undergo and withstand the shocks of adversity before it is entitled to the appellation.
  George Washington

Chapter 7
Focusing Forward

For several days I have scribbled on my notepad, jotting down various ideas on how to open this chapter. I kept coming back to a true story on how one man focused forward beyond what doctors told him was achievable. This man has great character, strength beyond comprehension and a focus forward on life that I believe will inspire you as much as it has me. This man is my husband, Ron.

First, you have to know my husband. He has a great big heart for dogs. Ron has never met a stray dog. He either brings the dog home with him or he is quick to find it a home. This is how he has acquired all his dogs throughout his entire life.

The second thing you have to know about Ron is that he has more energy than anyone I have ever met! He is like the energy bunny and I love it. Ron has always been very active since childhood (which his mom can attest to) and it makes him who he is.

Several years ago on a beautiful sunny day, Ron strapped on his roller blades and took his dog, Amber, to the park. As they did numerous times before, Ron had Amber on a leash and together they enjoyed some exercise and wonderful scenery. At last they were both worn out and ready to come home.

As they began their journey home, Amber saw a bunny rabbit and needless to say the chase was on! As Amber took off on a mad dash to catch the bunny, Ron followed. He didn't let go of the leash because they were next to a busy road and he was afraid if the rabbit ran into the road Amber would follow.

Over the next few minutes Amber, with Ron in tow, was chasing this little rabbit at speeds that would give NASCAR a run for its money.

As Ron and Amber came barreling down the sidewalk they saw a few bystanders ahead. At this point, Ron unconsciously dropped the leash. The bunny and Amber suddenly shot across the walkway right into Ron's path. Instead of rolling over Amber, Ron squatted down, picked Amber up and threw her off to the side to avoid further catastrophe. In the process of saving Amber, Ron went air born for several feet. His back took the brunt of the fall as he landed hard on the concrete sidewalk.

Several minutes later Ron opened his eyes and found himself lying on the ground in extreme pain. What followed over the next year is more than I can imagine.

After several doctor visits, Ron was told that his options were limited. Thankfully, doctors agreed to perform an exploratory surgery during which they found extensive nerve damage stemming from his spinal cord.

FOCUSING FORWARD

This damage completely impacted the use of Ron's knee and back.

Over the next year Ron was bound to crutches and unable to do any of the things that he loved to do. During this time, he lived in extreme pain. Because of the amount of pain and the level of damage, doctors actually considered amputating his leg from the knee down. Ron decided against this and began living on pain killers. After countless doctor visits, 13 surgeries, physical therapy, weekly knee injections and too many pain killers to count, Ron decided enough was enough. He set a goal. His goal was to walk again without any assistance, without any pain killers or weekly shots - one step at a time.

Ron made the choice to focus forward and he set the bar high. He decided that he would train for and complete a short distance triathlon, then an Olympic distance triathlon and ultimately an Ironman race. So you have a full picture of his goal, an Ironman race consists of a 2.4 mile swim, followed by a 112 mile bike ride, followed by a 26.2 mile run, all in one day. You must cross the finish line within 17 hours or you're disqualified.

Ron set his goal, planned out the details, began embracing an attitude of gratitude, surrounded himself with other Ironman athletes and audaciously began his journey of training for this grueling race.

His journey began slowly by getting into the water and trying to move his legs. Then he began kicking his legs, and finally, after several months, he had full movement of his legs. Next he started riding a stationary bike and eventually joined a local group of riders. He learned that the more he swam and biked, the less pain he felt.

Several months later he audaciously showed up at a local track and slowly began to walk. His eye was on the prize, he focused forward and believed that he could and would complete this Ironman race. He envisioned himself crossing that finish line with all of his family cheering him on.

I'm proud to tell you that this amazing man not only completed the Ironman race but has gone on to complete two others and is currently training for his fourth.

Today Ron still has pain from his accident but he makes the choice daily to persevere, to set SMART goals, to have outrageous enthusiasm and to walk audaciously through his fears while surrounding himself with a circle of influence that is so strong and powerful that each day is a true gift for him.

While we will all face difficulties, challenging times, sorrows and discouraging news, we must remember to focus forward and know that God is able to use our shortcomings, failures, sorrows and accidents to mold us into the people He designed us to be. Through these experiences God teaches us unforgettable lessons if we have an open mind and heart.

> *Have I not commanded you? Be strong and courageous. Do not be terrified; do not be discouraged, for the Lord your God will be with you wherever you go.*
> *Joshua 1:9*

By no means was that an easy year for Ron, but it was a year full of growth. Many days Ron didn't want to get out of bed, at times his pain got the best of him, but he would pick himself up off the floor, dust off his knees and focus forward.

This story embraces every component that we've discussed in this book thus far: setting ginormous goals, choosing to live each day with outrageous enthusiasm even in times when we don't feel like it, walking with an audacious spirit and living life to the fullest. My hope is that this story is an inspiration for all of us when we have a challenging day or season in our lives. My prayer is that we find the courage on this day to choose to live this life to the fullest and to know that God is on our side cheering for us.

> *And we know that in all things God works for the good of those who love him, who have been called according to his purpose.*
> *Romans 8:28*

Focusing forward means forgetting our past mistakes, letting go of our shortcomings and failures and looking ahead at all the possibilities that are out there for us. Keep your eyes focused forward. It does no good focusing on the past. When we focus on our past we direct our thoughts and efforts in the wrong direction. Instead, stand confident knowing that your future is bright and full of opportunities.

Often times we beat ourselves up over our past and replay our failures over and over and over. This destructive voice is Satan's work. The devil comes to steal your joy and fill you with negativity, insecurity and doubt. Rest assured that this is not our loving God talking to you. God has grand plans for you and wants you to know that you are His child and this is your time! God is waiting for each of us to turn the corner and break through that invisible wall called our past to experience joy, peace and abundant blessings.

All too often we forget that we are made in the image of God and that He believes in us. I know that each of you reading this message have unlimited, unleashed potential. It is when you see and believe in yourself that you will begin to fulfill your destiny. You don't need to know every detail of your future; you just need to begin by taking baby steps, putting one foot in front of the other, moving forward.

> ***Our greatest glory is not in never falling, but in rising every time we fall.***
> ***Confucius***

Don't let your past determine your future. Make the choice today to begin each day filled with forward focus resolve, knowing that you are successful and that God has abundant blessings in store for you.

Decide today what you want your future to look like. Maybe it's bringing that idea that you've had in the back of your mind to fruition, being more patient with your children, or becoming a better steward of your finances. I don't know what your deepest desires are, but I do know that putting them off until tomorrow may be too late. You have today to make a difference because tomorrow may never come. How many times have you heard someone say, "I'll start that diet tomorrow, I'll start exercising tomorrow, I'll look for a career that is fulfilling tomorrow"? Tomorrow never comes!

Make the decision today, right now, to live a life that is fulfilling and bold! Set an example that you will be proud to share with your children, your brothers, your sisters, your family and your friends. It's time today, on this day, to live your life out loud! It is your turn!

Chapter 8
Predictors of Success

When I was little I used to think that success only happened to people who came from money, had high intelligence or had friends of influence.

I've since learned that success comes from a lot of hard work and many failures along the way. I also have learned that where there is a failure, there is a success.

- Mary Kay Ash hit the glass ceiling in her corporate sales job which resulted in her taking early retirement. She went on to launch her cosmetic company which now enriches the lives of over 1.7 million women in more than 33 countries.

- Thomas Edison invented many devices that changed our world forever. He stated, "If I find 10,000 ways something won't work, I haven't failed. I am not discouraged, because every wrong attempt discarded is another step forward."

- Oprah Winfrey was fired at the age of 22 from a reporting job in Baltimore, Maryland, because she was a "bad" reporter. She went on to co-host "People Are Talking" and later established The Oprah Winfrey show, winning numerous awards.

> *Would you like me to give you a formula for success? It's quite simple, really. Double your rate of failure. You are thinking of failure as the enemy of success. But it isn't at all. You can be discouraged by failure or you can learn from it, so go ahead and make mistakes. Make all you can. Because remember that's where you will find success.*
>   *Thomas J. Watson*

For many years I feared failure without realizing that was how God teaches us lessons. I don't know about you, but I apparently only learn things the hard way.

It is in these times of failing forward where we learn lessons that help us grow and develop into who we are designed to be. While we may see a situation as a failure,

God uses it as preparation for the next step in life. God sees the whole picture where we may only see a small glimpse. It is therefore necessary to have a file full of failures so that we may have an even greater file cabinet full of successes.

> *Success isn't permanent, and failure isn't fatal.*
> *Mike Ditka*

I recently read in Dan Miller's *48 Days To Creative Income* that there are five predictors of success that he identifies and all of them lead back to focusing forward.

1. Passion

2. Determination

3. Talent

4. Self-Discipline

5. Faith

Let's take a closer look at these five predictors of success.

Passion: A person with passion is a person who can set goals. Without them, you can have no clear direction and will drift along the road of circumstances. Live intentionally.

Bill Gates was able to build Microsoft and become the richest man in the world because he was passionate about his vision of putting a computer on every desk.

Determination: Without a clear purpose, any obstacle will send a person in a new direction. Without determination a person can easily be lured away from the destined path. But with determination you can establish priorities that will guide you through even the most challenging and unexpected circumstances.

Clara Barton was determined to help wounded Civil War soldiers as well as abolish slavery and establish women's rights. With her determination she helped establish the American Red Cross in 1881.

Talent: No one has talent in every area, but everyone has talent. Discover where you rise to the top. What are those things you love to do, and would do whether or not you got paid? Sometimes we discover that our first sense of "calling" is guided more by others expectations than as a true reflection of our strongest areas of competence.

At the young age of seven and a half, Beethoven gave his first known public performance. His talent for music was constantly enhanced throughout his life through mentors and education.

Self-Discipline: Without self-discipline, a person can easily be swayed by others. Self-discipline is the foundation that makes the other predictors work. Knowing those predictors is the initial step, but acting on them always requires self-discipline.

PREDICTORS OF SUCCESS

Maya Angelou persisted in writing even when others discouraged her. Today she enjoys a significant yearly income for her published materials.

Faith: Even with everything lining up logically, there still comes that leap of faith into the unknown. You cannot reach new lands if you keep one foot on the shore.

Mother Teresa had unwavering faith that changed hundreds of thousands of lives during her lifetime. She always gave credit to God for her accomplishments and viewed herself as an instrument in helping the poor.

These five predictors of success are not based on intelligence, family lineage or current circumstances; they are all based on the gifts, skills and abilities that you already have. You have the ability to establish a new path not only for yourself but for others. It takes one small step at a time.

The difference between a successful person and others is not a lack of strength, not a lack of knowledge, but rather in a lack of will.
Vincent T. Lombardi

I recently read an article in Woman's World magazine that confirmed the power of turning failures into successes. Tory Johnson, workplace contributor for *Good Morning America,* kicked off an initiative called Job Club. This club created a venue where those looking for work could get together with others who were in the same situation. They would limit the group from five to 12 people in order to ensure diversity and also allow enough time for each member to talk openly and freely. This group of individuals had lost their jobs due to corporate downsizing, not fitting the corporate environment or because of unmet expectations. Each person struggled with feelings of failure.

At first, during their weekly meeting they began by talking openly about their struggles, challenges and emotional turmoil. As they worked through their grief, they began seeing future successes.

They started their meetings by pointing out each other's strengths, gifts, abilities and skills. They brought in guest speakers and business coaches to talk about building a resume, interviewing skills and current career trends. They also hosted a "beauty" day where they had image consultants talk with them about the importance of looking and feeling good from the inside out. All of these success efforts helped re-establish a healthy, positive self-confidence.

Within four months of beginning this club all 12 people landed jobs! Now that's the power of turning failures into successes.

> *Seventy percent of success in life is showing up.*
> *Woody Allen*

Like this group, I needed someone to breathe belief into me after I left corporate America. I vividly remember leaving my job with 14 years of belongings on a single cart. As I pushed the little cart I kept thinking, "Fourteen years and this is all I have to show for it?" I was sad and didn't have a lot of confidence as I headed down the dark, empty hallway to my car. I am grateful to my inner circle for believing in me when I didn't believe in myself. They helped me learn that although I lost my job I had years of education and experiences to share and use to encourage others. I can look back now at my failures and see how they have turned into successes.

Recently I had the incredible opportunity to speak to a group of 50-75 women about living a Ginormous, Outrageous, Audacious Life! These women needed someone to breath belief into them. They were facing everything from fighting addictions, to being jobless, to living on the streets with their children. If I hadn't lost my job and experienced emotional turmoil, I would have never walked this path and been able to encourage these beautiful women.

I think the word failure has such a negative connotation. The Merriam Webster Dictionary defines the word failure, in part, as a lack of success. I believe we need a new definition that claims the word failure as a step to success! We fail forward into our successes! Don't be afraid of making mistakes and failing. I promise you that the lessons learned from failing far outweigh the dent to our ego.

Success is a journey, not a destination.
Ben Sweetland

Chapter 9

Paying It Forward

> *A person starts to live when he can live outside himself.*
> *Albert Einstein*

You may be asking yourself, what on earth does paying it forward have to do with living a ginormous, outrageous, audacious life?

I believe that once we're setting ginormous goals, living with outrageous enthusiasm and audaciously walking through fears, it's our responsibility to share these gifts with others. Paying it forward may be passing along this book to someone in need, it may be a friendly smile, or it could be a warm greeting to someone you pass on the street. You have the power to influence others. If you can change just one person's life by showing them that life can be ginormous, outrageous and audacious, then you've given the most precious gift you can give.

My entire purpose in writing this book is to pay it forward by showing you that you have amazing power to direct your life! I've been blessed to learn these lessons throughout my life and it is my turn to pay it forward to as many of you as possible.

Think back to the good deeds that others have done for you. Do you remember feeling special and important when someone thought about you and then acted on it? Paying it forward means bringing these good deeds full-circle and doing something nice for someone else. Many times you'll never even know the impact that you have on another person.

One year, Ron and I decided that we wanted to pay it forward to an assisted living facility in our area. It was February so we thought it would be the perfect month to show our love and respect to these amazing elders. Ron and I went to the store a few days before Valentine's Day and purchased 175 red roses. We took them home and placed them in large trash cans to keep them fresh. We then created Valentine's Day cards, like the ones you got in grade school with fun little messages. We paper punched each one of the cards, strung red ribbon through each card and tied them individually onto each rose.

The day before Valentine's Day we set out with all of these roses and cards to the assisted living facility. We placed the roses into baskets (a little prettier than the trash cans) and made our way through the facility wishing all our elderly friends a happy Valentine's Day.

Although we were doing it to make the residents feel special, I can tell you it was they who enriched our lives tenfold. I could write pages and pages about how many of our new friends shared that they hadn't received a flower on Valentine's Day for over a decade. Some of these men and woman had never received a red rose in their life. For some the last flower received was from a spouse who had passed away years prior. Story after story was such a gift to Ron and me.

That's the funny thing about giving; you're the one who receives the gift in the end.

Paying it forward reminds me of Teflon® pans - the ones where food slides right off the pan onto your plate. I try to envision myself like a Teflon® pan, making sure the blessings that come my way slide off of me and turn into a gift for others. If we could be more Teflon®-like people we could truly make a difference. I genuinely believe that by helping just one person at a time we can make a significant revolution in this world from country to country and continent to continent.

It only takes one small act, one small word or one small work to pay it forward. You never know how many lives you will touch.

I have to share one more story about a recent pay it forward idea. Last week I went through the Starbucks' drive-thru, handed the barista a $20 bill and asked her to treat as many customers behind me as the money would cover. I just had to watch peoples' reactions so I pulled into a parking lot hidden by trees next door and waited.

Every driver's initial response was shock as they looked over their shoulder expecting to see someone familiar. What came next brought me pure joy. Each and every driver smiled. I love to smile almost as much as I love to see others smile. I was humbled as I finally drove away thinking about the little sliver of sunshine that those people felt that day.

You cannot live a ginormous, outrageous, audacious life without paying it forward! It is the essence of how we are wired.

> *The value of a man should be seen in what he gives and not in what he is able to receive.*
> *Albert Einstein*

> *From everyone who has been given much, much will be demanded; and from the one who has been entrusted with much, much more will be asked.*
> *Luke 12:48b*

I once heard someone say, "It's the heart that makes the mark." In life we use so many words but what people truly remember are your actions and how you made them feel.

You may remember a few years ago when Oprah Winfrey launched a paying it forward challenge. She gave over 300 people $1,000 each and challenged them to come up with inspiring and creative ways to help others. The stories were so touching that it made hundreds and thousands of others turn around and pay it forward. What an inspiration!

PAYING IT FORWARD

I want to share with you some of the paying it forward stories that I've read recently.

1. One group of six friends pooled money together to buy gift cards from a local grocery store. They randomly handed the gift cards out to people they met on the street. This local grocery store found out and matched their contributions so they had double the amount of gift cards to hand out.

2. One person donated books, clothing and school supplies to a school in Africa where the children walk more than two hours to and from school each day with no shoes. Though the school experiences extreme poverty, they now have a 98% attendance rate.

3. One couple took a group of little girls who lived in a homeless shelter out for a night. They took them shopping to buy new outfits, to a restaurant for dinner and then to a play.

4. One group of friends were filling up their car at a local gas station where they overheard a single mother tell her two year-old son that she only had $2 for gas so he couldn't have any food. They not only paid for this mother's full tank of gas and food for her son, but they also stayed for several hours filling up other's gas tanks.

Kindness is a language which the deaf can hear and the blind can see.
Mark Twain

Paying it forward has a ripple effect. Once you begin paying it forward other's want to jump in and join you. I've seen store owner's match dollar for dollar efforts, I've seen neighbor's tend to other neighbor's yards after being on the receiving end and I've seen tolls paid for countless drivers as they continue paying for those behind them in the toll lines.

What would it take to start your own pay it forward challenge? Remember, paying it forward is not about money, it is merely showing kindness to others. I guarantee that it will forever change your life as you take others along with you!

No kind action ever stops with itself. One kind action leads to another. Good example is followed. A single act of kindness throws out roots in all directions, and the roots spring up and make new trees. The greatest work that kindness does to others is that it makes them kind themselves.
Amelia Earhart

Chapter 10

Your Unwritten Chapter

As we come to a close in this book, I want to ask YOU what your next chapter looks like. This is a defining moment in your life where you can choose to close this book (at the end of this chapter, of course) and continue life as is, or you can choose today, this very day, to write a new beginning.

I, too, am making a choice to write a chapter that is unknown, unwritten and full of "what if" types of questions. I know that I'm willing to listen to God's voice and put one foot in front of the other even though I don't know the ending. What I am certain of is making the daily choice to walk through those walls of fear and persevere. I believe God wants to bring out the best in each and every one of us. If we just move one step at a time He will carry us where our feet can no longer walk. He will take us on a journey that will forever change our lives and the lives of those around us.

GINORMOUS, OUTRAGEOUS, AUDACIOUS LIVING!

We each get one shot at this life and my prayer is that we can all look back and say, without hesitation, that we journeyed well. That we used every single gift, skill and ability that we were given; that we set ginormous goals; that we lived with outrageous enthusiasm; that we audaciously faced our fears and came out on the other side, taking others with us.

> *When I stand before God at the end of my life, I would hope that I would not have a single bit of talent left, and could say, "I used everything you gave me."*
>
>   *Erma Bombeck*

> *Remember, the road to success is not straight,*
> *There is a curve called failure,*
> *A loop called confusion,*
> *Speed bumps called friends,*
> *Red lights called enemies,*
> *Caution lights called family,*
> *And you will have flats called jobs.*
>
> *But, if you have a spare called determination,*
> *An engine called perseverance,*
> *Insurance called faith,*

And a driver named God,
You will make it to a place called success.

Yes, it is difficult to say what is impossible,
for the dream of yesterday is the hope of today
and reality of tomorrow.

Happiness keeps you sweet.
Trials keep you strong.
Sorrows keep you human.
Failures keep you humble.

Success keeps you glowing.
But only God keeps you going,
because you are special!

Remember, we can do all things
as it relates to success through our God
who gives strength to all of us.

Yes, the power to hold on in spite of everything,
the power to endure, this is the winner's quality
and the road to success.

National Chaplain

Worksheets

SMART GOAL SHEETS
Pages 83-87

TEAR-OUT DAILY INSPIRATIONS
Pages 89-123

GIFTS, SKILLS, ABILITIES WORKSHEET
Pages 125-128

CIRCLE OF INFLUENCE WORKSHEET
Pages 129-131

SMART GOAL SHEET

DATE:

MY GOAL IS:

SPECIFIC:

MEASURABLE:

ACTION PLAN:

REACH HIGH:

TIMELINE:

SMART GOAL SHEET

DATE:

MY GOAL IS:

SPECIFIC:

MEASURABLE:

ACTION PLAN:

REACH HIGH:

TIMELINE:

SMART GOAL SHEET

DATE:

MY GOAL IS:

SPECIFIC:

MEASURABLE:

ACTION PLAN:

REACH HIGH:

TIMELINE:

TEAR-OUT DAILY INSPIRATIONS

With definite goals you release your own power, and things start happening.
   Zig Ziglar

Examine yourself; discover where your true chance of greatness lies.
Seize that chance and let no power or persuasion deter you from your task.
   Schoolmaster in Chariots of Fire

Each one should use whatever gift he has received to serve others, faithfully administering God's grace in its various forms.
   1 Peter 4:10

And we know that in all things God works for the good of those who love him, who have been called according to his purpose.
   Romans 8:28

When you get into a tight place and everything goes against you, till it seems as though you could not hold on a minute longer, never give up then, for that is just the place and time that the tide will turn.
   Harriet Beecher Stowe

Consider it pure joy, my brothers, whenever you face trials of many kinds, because you know that the testing of your faith develops perseverance. Perseverance must finish its work so that you may be mature and complete, not lacking anything.
   James 1:2-4

Nothing great was ever achieved without enthusiasm.
    Ralph Waldo Emerson

Blessed is the man who perseveres under trial, because when he has stood the test, he will receive the crown of life that God has promised to those who love him.
    James 1:12

I have learned that success is to be measured not so much by the position that one has reached in life as by the obstacles which he has overcome while trying to succeed.
    Booker T. Washington

"For I know the plans I have for you," declares the Lord, "plans to prosper you and not to harm you, plans to give you hope and a future."
  Jeremiah 29:11

Be persistent in pursuing your dreams.
  Oprah Winfrey

We have different gifts, according to the grace given us. If a man's gift is prophesying, let him use it in proportion to his faith. If it is serving, let him serve; if it is teaching, let him teach; if it is encouraging, let him encourage; if it is contributing to the needs of others, let him give generously; if it is leadership, let him govern diligently; if it is showing mercy, let him do it cheerfully.
  Romans 12:6-8

If God is for us, who can be against us?
   Romans 8:31b

The longest journey begins with a single step.
   Chinese proverb

May he give you the desire of your heart and make all your plans succeed. We will shout for joy when you are victorious and will lift up our banners in the name of our God. May the Lord grant all your requests.
   Psalm 20:4-5

Whatever the mind can conceive and believe, you can achieve.
   Mary Kay Ash

Life is a mirror and will reflect back to the thinker what he thinks into it.
  Ernest Holmes

If you have any encouragement from being united with Christ, if any comfort from his love, if any fellowship with the Spirit, if any tenderness and compassion, then make my joy complete by being like-minded, having the same love, being one in spirit and purpose. Do nothing out of selfish ambition or vain conceit, but in humility consider others better than yourselves. Each of you should look not only to your own interests, but also to the interests of others. Your attitude should be the same as that of Christ Jesus.
  Philippians 2:1-5

We are what we repeatedly do. Excellence, then, is not an act, but a habit.
  Aristotle

A cheerful heart is good medicine, but a crushed spirit dries up the bones.
  Proverbs 17:22

Fear defeats more people than any other one thing in the world.
  Ralph Waldo Emerson

The thief comes only to steal and kill and destroy; I have come that they may have life, and have it to the full.
  John 10:10

You can conquer almost any fear if you will only make up your mind to do so. For remember, fear doesn't exist anywhere except in the mind.
   Dale Carnegie

One loyal friend is worth ten thousand relatives.
   Euripides

There is no fear in love. But perfect love drives out fear, because fear has to do with punishment. The one who fears is not made perfect in love.
   1 John 4:18

You gain strength, courage and confidence by every experience in which you really stop to look fear in the face. You must do the thing which you think you cannot do.
   Eleanor Roosevelt

"I took you from the ends of the earth, from its farthest corners I called you. I said, 'You are my servant'; I have chosen you and have not rejected you. So do not fear, for I am with you; do not be dismayed, for I am your God. I will strengthen you and help you; I will uphold you with my righteous right hand."
   Isaiah 41:9-10

My friends are my estate.
   Emily Dickinson

Anybody who believes in something without reservation believes that this thing is right and should be, has the stamina to meet obstacles and overcome them.
  Golda Meir

If the Lord delights in a man's way, he makes his steps firm; though he stumble, he will not fall, for the Lord upholds him with his hand.
  Psalm 37:23-24

Grief can take care of itself, but to get the full value of a joy you must have somebody to divide it with.
  Mark Twain

A friend loves at all times, and a brother is born for adversity.
   Proverbs 17:17

True happiness consists not in the multitude of friends, but in their worth and choice.
   Samuel Johnston

After David had finished talking with Saul, Jonathan became one in spirit with David, and he loved him as himself. From that day Saul kept David with him and did not let him return to his father's house. And Jonathan made a covenant with David because he loved him as himself. Jonathan took off the robe he was wearing and gave it to David, along with his tunic, and even his sword, his bow and his belt.
   1 Samuel 18:1-4

He who walks with the wise grows wise, but a companion of fools suffers harm.
   Proverbs 13:20

Thus nature has no love for solitude, and always leans, as it were, on some support; and the sweetest support is found in the most intimate friendship.
   Cicero

Associate yourself with men of good quality if you esteem your own reputation; for 'tis better to be alone than in bad company.
   George Washington

True friendship is a plant of slow growth, and must undergo and withstand the shocks of adversity before it is entitled to the appellation.
   George Washington

Have I not commanded you? Be strong and courageous. Do not be terrified; do not be discouraged, for the Lord your God will be with you wherever you go.
   Joshua 1:9

And we know that in all things God works for the good of those who love him, who have been called according to his purpose.
   Romans 8:28

Our greatest glory is not in never falling, but in rising every time we fall.
   Confucius

Would you like me to give you a formula for success? It's quite simple, really. Double your rate of failure. You are thinking of failure as the enemy of success. But it isn't at all. You can be discouraged by failure or you can learn from it, so go ahead and make mistakes. Make all you can. Because remember that's where you will find success.
   Thomas J. Watson

Success isn't permanent, and failure isn't fatal.
   Mike Ditka

The difference between a successful person and others is not a lack of strength, not a lack of knowledge, but rather in a lack of will.
  Vincent T. Lombardi

Seventy percent of success in life is showing up.
  Woody Allen

Success is a journey, not a destination.
  Ben Sweetland

A person starts to live when he can live outside himself.
  Albert Einstein

The value of a man should be seen in what he gives and not in what he is able to receive.
   Albert Einstein

Kindness is a language which the deaf can hear and the blind can see.
   Mark Twain

No kind action ever stops with itself. One kind action leads to another. Good example is followed. A single act of kindness throws out roots in all directions, and the roots spring up and make new trees. The greatest work that kindness does to others is that it makes them kind themselves.
   Amelia Earhart

When I stand before God at the end of my life, I would hope that I would not have a single bit talent left, and could say, "I used everything you gave me."
   Erma Bombeck

Courage is fear holding on a minute longer.
   George S. Patton

Remember, the road to success is not straight,
There is a curve called failure,
A loop called confusion,
Speed bumps called friends,
Red lights called enemies,
Caution lights called family,
And you will have flats called jobs.

But, if you have a spare called determination,
An engine called perseverance,
Insurance called faith,
And a driver named God,
You will make it to a place called success.

National Chaplain

GIFTS, SKILLS, ABILITIES WORKSHEET

Take some time to reflect inward and identify your gifts, skills and abilities. Being able to identify your gifts, skills and abilities will allow you to live your life to its fullest potential. Maybe you'll discover a new career opportunity or maybe you will realize that you can pick up a new hobby that will add creativity and excitement back into your life. Here are some questions to get you started.

1. Think back to your childhood, what did you enjoy doing? Examples: playing school and you were the teacher, watching insects and animals and learning about them or maybe you took things apart and enjoyed fixing them.

_____
_____
_____
_____
_____
_____
_____
_____
_____
_____

2. Ask your close family members and friends what they see as your gifts. Examples: good at encouraging others, very creative and artistic or maybe a good listener.

_____
_____
_____
_____
_____
_____
_____

3. What do you do in your pastime, in the evenings, on the weekends? Examples: took an art class, entertain friends and family, try cooking new recipes.

_____
_____
_____
_____
_____
_____
_____

GIFTS, SKILLS, ABILITIES WORKSHEET

4. What are your hobbies? Examples: work on restoring cars, painting, playing on an athletic team.

_____
_____
_____
_____
_____
_____

5. Take a few minutes and close your eyes. Let your mind wonder and relax. If money were not an issue, what you would enjoy doing the most? What makes your heart race with excitement? Examples: Hosting and planning parties, telling stories to friends and family or making personalized purses.

_____
_____
_____
_____
_____
_____

GINORMOUS, OUTRAGEOUS, AUDACIOUS LIVING!

Take a look and review your answers. Do you see patterns? Do you notice that some of your answers show up several times?

For example, maybe you notice that you like being with people the majority of the time. What could you do to maximize your gift of people skills? If you notice that you enjoy working with your hands, what could you do to embrace your motor skills?

This is your time to identify your gifts, skills and abilities. By taking the time to do this you are opening doors of opportunity to live that ginormous, outrageous, audacious life!

What are your buried treasures? No one can truly grasp your inner self except for you. This is the key! Once you figure this out, then you can move forward maximizing those specific and unique gifts, skills and abilities.

CIRCLE OF INFLUENCE WORKSHEET

This is a great activity to take a few minutes and identify your friends, which group they fall in, and if you're spending a healthy amount of time with each group. You may realize that it is necessary to adjust who you're spending your time with.

A healthy balance within your circle of influence is spending 10% of your time with sprinters, 10% of your time with marathoners and 80% of your time with your inner circle.

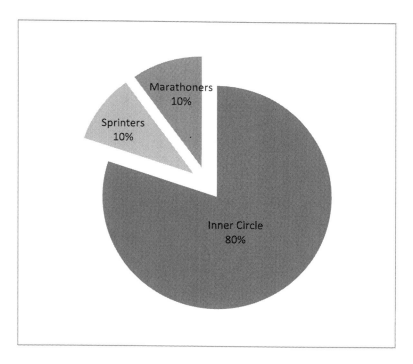

Sprinters - These friendships may be more short distance or for a season. It's more of a fun, light-hearted, conversational group of friends.

Marathoners - These friends you've had for years. You've grown up together; they know your family and have been with you through many seasons or marathons.

Inner circle - These friends you can count on one hand. This group knows everything about you from your greatest achievements to your most embarrassing moments. They encourage you and are honest enough to tell you the good, the bad and the ugly.

Use the chart on the next page to see if you have a healthy balance within your circle of influence.

CIRCLE OF INFLUENCE WORKSHEET

SPRINTERS 10% of your time	MARATHONERS 10% of your time	INNER CIRCLE 80% of your time

Notes

---

[1] Dan Miller, 48 Days To the Work You Love (Nashville: B&H, 2007),p.77.

[2] Dan Miller, 48 Days To the Work You Love (Nashville: B&H, 2007),p.56.

Made in the USA
Charleston, SC
24 August 2010